THE

THE SKY OVER WALES

by Siân James

with illustrations by Pat Gregory

HONNO *AUTOBIOGRAPHY*

Published by Honno
'Ailsa Craig', Heol y Cawl, Dinas Powys
Bro Morgannwg CF64 4AH

First impression 1997

British Library Cataloguing in Publication Data

A catalogue record for this book is available from the British Library

ISBN 1 870206 28 2

*Published with the financial support
of the Arts Council of Wales*

Design and layout by Chris Lee Design
Printed by Qualitex Printing Limited, Cardiff

My maternal grandmother died when I was just over two years old. I can't quite remember her, but I have a definite memory of her death, or at least of my mother in a long black mourning dress.

I remember my mother, then, as long and thin - she became plump soon afterwards - and the dress was starkly black with one large button at the throat. I suppose I must have been on her lap and asking, 'Beth yw hwnna?' (What is that?) and I suppose she must have said, 'Bwtwn,' (button) many times without satisfying me, so that she finally said, 'Mother-of-pearl,' which I demanded to hear over and over again, enchanted by this new sound. For years the word used to give me a shock of pleasure.

I remember the garden in spring, a blaze of tall yellow daffodils around a tree stump in the middle of the grass. I remember crying, perhaps screaming and kicking, because my mother seemed intent on cutting them all down. I remember her lifting me up and saying, in Welsh, 'Aren't you willing for me to take them to Mamgu's grave?' I calmed down at the sadness and ser-iousness of her voice. *But I wasn't willing.*

. . . . .

I remember shapes and textures, sounds and smells: the cold, brown-patterned lino in my bedroom, the fluffy rug in my mother's bedroom which tickled the soles of my feet, the splash of water poured into a bowl, the scratch of face flannel, the sting of soap in the eyes, nice frock that fitted or frock that was hot and tight, the kettle hissing on the fire, the smell of tea as the water was poured into the shiny brown pot, a pain in my chest as I screamed about something.

I can't remember my mother ever smacking me, but sometimes she would shake me, which made all my thoughts tumble about.

I remember learning about pain. One night in bed my cheeks were burning and my mother said I had tooth-ache. I remember feeling very surprised, because the pain seemed outside me on the pillow; toothache was horrible. Sometimes I had a different pain; a little fire when I swallowed. My mother said it was 'gwddwg tost' which didn't sound too bad, but when my father said I had a throat infection it seemed frightening enough to cry about. Once when I was in bed with a sore throat I suddenly vomited all over the bedclothes. 'Why didn't you tell me you wanted to be sick?' my mother asked me. But I didn't *want* to be sick. Who could ever *want* to be sick?

The worst illness I remember was mumps. Though I was so hot, I had to wear a silk scarf round my ears and I thought my face was turning into a turnip.

When I was ill my mother had lovely cold hands and a nice soft voice, but I wasn't allowed to call her too often.

. . . . .

Tea-leaves in a warmed pot was my favourite smell, though I didn't like the taste of tea. One morning I pulled the teapot towards me not knowing that my mother had already filled it, and the hot tea cascaded over me. I wasn't badly hurt, probably because I was so well cocooned in chilprufe vest, liberty bodice and lumpy, hand-knitted jumper. My chest was only slightly pink but I was given a piece of chocolate, because my mother felt guilty for turning her back on me, I suppose; she was more upset than I was.

Whenever I saw my naked body, it seemed unfamiliar and alien, my bottom, of course, both hilarious and shaming, and though I liked my belly-button a lot, I felt much more at ease with myself in my little jumper and pinafore dress.

. . . . .

My sister Mair, ten years older than I was, doted on me and used to take me round the village in a pushchair, encouraging me to show off by reciting whole books of nursery rhymes to anyone who'd listen. At a Christmas concert when I was three, I was put on the stage to recite some short poem and refused to get down until I'd gone through my whole repertoire. I still remember the applause I got. Particularly when I was carried off at last.

My sister Bob thought I was spoilt and big-headed - she was right - and always took it upon herself to keep me in my place. She and I shared a bedroom - and a bed - and she drew up a set of rules which I had to repeat every night before I went to sleep: I wasn't to boast, I wasn't to tell lies, I wasn't to be cheeky. The last, very important, rule was that I was to keep to my own side of the bed and *not stick my bottom out.*

She also insisted that we go through six or seven prayers every night. The first were quite short, but they got progressively longer and ended with an improvised prayer for us, our family, our extended family, our teachers, our friends, the parents and grandparents of our friends - indeed, everyone we knew - and could well last twenty minutes.

My brother Ifan, fifteen years older than I, was studying for his Higher School Certificate, and later his college exams, and used to be maddened by these loudly-intoned ramblings and used to shout downstairs, 'Mam, those children are still praying'. If he didn't get any response from her, he'd rush in and smack us.

Ifan was a handsome young man and fastidious in his habits. He couldn't put up with me because, according to him, I was always sticky. He was fonder of my sister Bob.

I was just three when he was made a prefect at the County School and my mother used to persuade me to say 'Good morning, prefect', when he left the house. I felt foolish saying it. I've never been much good at flattery.

My mother was warm and loving, though she could get irritable when she had too much to do, and I suppose that was much of the time. Even in my earliest memories I'm aware of the tired, cross, morning mother and the happier afternoon version when she had a few minutes to sit down to read to me and let me read to her. She used to get fashion magazines from Barkers and Derry and Toms and when she'd finished with them, would let me cut out - with a pair of very blunt scissors - the strange emaciated ladies, some in corsets and bust-bodices, some with dead foxes draped around their shoulders.

She was always pleased when I used the po without fuss, though she was never cross on the many occasions when I wet the bed; warm and sensuous at first but then very cold.

One of my best memories is of my mother ironing, her mind obviously on something else, and humming; not a tune exactly but a long, contented string of sounds, not unlike a bee in the flowers.

My father was the headmaster of the elementary school in Llanbadarn, which was almost a mile away from the Waun where we lived. I can't remember that he ever showed much interest in me until I was six or seven, when he began to suspect that I was rather clever. He used to shut himself away from the family whenever he could to listen to his wireless set, and whenever I intruded upon him, 'Run away, gel fach,' he'd say. My father was English, his parents from Somerset, but he was persuaded by my mother to speak some sort of basic Welsh to his children when they were young, which must have made communication rather difficult. He studied Welsh for years but never managed to speak it fluently, though his vocabulary was extensive. Many people, parents of the children he taught, for instance, didn't realise he couldn't speak Welsh because he understood everything they had to tell him and would then raise his hand and say, 'Popeth yn iawn,' (That'll be fine), which always satisfied them perfectly.

Unlike my mother's family, my father wasn't artistic, didn't exaggerate, didn't weave stories. But he said what he meant and would do what he promised.

We were a two pushchair family. One of them was a small, light one, not too unlike the modern type, the other was a luxury carriage, much larger, its bodywork covered in crimson plush ornamented with braids and tassels which wouldn't have looked out of place in Queen Victoria's nursery. I seem to remember a bone or ivory handle. It was so grand, so out of our sphere, that I think my mother must have been given it by a Lady Lloyd, the squire's wife in the village where I was born, who was, it seems, munificent in her bounty to the deserving peasantry. I'm afraid I liked it far better than the other which my mother favoured as being easier to push. Luckily, my sister Mair always took me out in the resplendent red Roller. One evening when we were on the other side of the village, one of its ancient wheels rolled off and we processed home, Mair carrying me, her friend Joan lugging the pushchair and my sister Bob carrying the wheel. It was very exciting.

Until I was seven or eight years old, we didn't have a bathroom or even an inside tap, all our water having to be fetched from a pump out on the road. This must have been a great hardship to my father and my brother whose daily task it was to fill the 'stên' and buckets, but I loved following them to watch the water cascading out.

Turn on a tap and you get a decent but domesticated flow, but from a pump, a blue, sparkling, metallic-looking column which sloshes and crashes and splashes into a pail or pitcher. (And if you lean over and put your hand under it, you're a very naughty girl, but it tingles right up to your teeth.)

. . . . .

A lovely ꜱᴛᴏʀy: my first stars. It was after a Christmas concert in Llanbadarn, I think I was two or possibly three. My father was carrying me out of the chapel vestry, I was probably half-asleep. It was very cold, very dark, and looking up I suddenly saw the huge spread of black sky, the white moon and all the dazzling company of stars. I must have gasped because I remember my mother explaining to the others that it was my first time out in the night.

I've had my share of star-filled nights since, with brash boys and peerless young men. But there were never stars like those first stars.

When I was three or three and a half I used to be taken to Llanbadarn school on an occasional Wednesday afternoon by our little maid, Annie, who had the afternoon off and who lived near the school. I was left in the Infants' class in the all-too-capable hands of Miss Bronwen Jenkins who had black, stiffly permed hair flattened to her head in a series of mathematically precise waves, a rather harsh voice, and dark, watchful eyes. My sister Bob adored Miss Jenkins, imitating her expressions and quoting her frequently, which may have been the reason for my decided coolness towards her. I much preferred the rocking horse - dappled grey, red flaring nostrils, bottle-green eyes - and the big Noah's Ark. (And it was just as well that I made the most of them when I was a visiting under-five, because the regular pupils were seldom allowed to play with them.)

The introduction to school life proved of great value. I observed that there were two types of children in the class, the meek, who were ignored, and the bold, who were tolerated until they went too far and had to stand in the corner. I resolved to be bold but cautious.

. . . . .

My mother was surprised when I said that her new bowl was indigo and black. (It was shiny and black on the outside and indigo on the inside and it cost one and sixpence.) When Mrs Davies-y-Mans comes to tea, my mother asks me to tell her what colour it is and I say blue and black and my mother tuts and pushes me a bit. I don't like Mrs Davies-y-Mans because she puts her face towards you for a kiss and her cheeks are furry and powdery but you have to kiss her because she's a visitor. She calls my mother Mrs Davies and my mother calls her Mrs Davies, so I take my piece of cake to the kitchen and Annie and I play visitors and call each other Mrs Davies. And then I learn more colours from my paintbox.

I tell Annie the colour of my mother's new bowl - indigo - and she lets me drink some dark tea from her saucer. I don't like it much, but I make a polite face. My mother is always begging me to be polite, even using the English word 'polite', so that I know it's very important. Like giving Mrs Davies-y-Mans a kiss when I don't want to.

· · · · ·

Annie, our little maid, lived in, remaining with us for two to three years from the time she left school at fourteen. She had curly reddish hair, very pale blue eyes, a round pale face, skin that always seemed to be moist and a low, rumbling voice. Even at two or three I knew she wasn't bright and I'm sorry to say that I never felt entirely comfortable with her, though she used to let me ride on her back when she was on her knees washing the floor. My mother was often cross with her - she was not only slow at her work but would often forget what she was supposed to be doing - and this made me uncomfortable. I wanted her to stick up for herself, but she never did.

On one occasion, though, she and my sister Mair had a fight over some mangling they were supposed to be doing together. They were pulling each other's hair, and though I loved Mair, I remember feeling very pleased that Annie was fighting back for once.

. . . . .

Before I went to bed I did pi-pi in front of the fire in a little green enamel po. I liked to say the word enamel but I thought po was a baby word. My Auntie Siân called it 'yr articlyn' - the article - but I didn't like that either.

Our Welsh was peppered with English words and I think they made a particular impression on me. (My mother talked English to my father and Welsh to her children, so perhaps I thought it a more grown-up language.) We had three bedrooms on the second floor of the house, which was always called 'thetopfloor'. I wasn't allowed to go up to 'thetopfloor' on my own in case I fell down the second flight of stairs, which wasn't carpeted like the first but covered with shiny brown oilcloth. When I started to draw houses they weren't the usual two up, two down, but had a strange accretion on them which was, of course, 'thetopfloor', which in my mind had all the glamour of a penthouse flat.

I loved the word 'mackintosh'. Sometimes my mother called it a 'cot law' - raincoat - but I always corrected her.

I was always delighted by words that tripped about and chimed. 'Ding dong bell, pussy's in the well', 'Ring-a-ring o' roses', 'Pat-a-cake, pat-a-cake', 'Pwsi meri mew, ple collaist ti dy flew?' 'Duw cariad yw', 'Ups-a-daisy'.

Words intended to inspire a thrill of fear - 'Bogey man', 'Mari Wen', and 'Here comes the chopper to chop off your head' - only excited me. But other, more mysterious words, 'the Sandman', for instance, held real terror.

I was also nervous of medical terms - adhesions, stroke, sanatorium, poultice, double pneumonia - and my mother and her younger sister, Auntie Maggie, offered me a thesaurus of those; everyone they knew suffered heart attacks, seizures or strokes, though sometimes it was only 'a pull', another very sinister word. I listened to their House of Horror conversations in fascinated dread.

When I was two or three, one of my favourite games was to knock on the big brass doorknocker on the front door, pretending to be a visitor. It was Annie who usually answered and she used to say, 'Someone to see you, Mrs Davis,' while I followed her through the long passage into the kitchen to be greeted rather, or sometimes *very*, wearily by my mother.

The game went wrong on one occasion. My sister Mair was home from school, perhaps expecting one of her friends, and seeing me, slammed the heavy door in my face. I tried to push my hand in to stop it shutting and the tip of my middle finger was caught and sliced off; I remember seeing it hanging on by a thread of skin. I must have howled like a demon because my father arrived and carried me to the back door where there was a bucket of clean water from the pump, and from sheer panic, I suppose, swished my finger round and round in it. I remember the water turning tomato red.

I thought all my blood had come out, but it hadn't. I was still quite firm and solid as my mother sat me on the kitchen table and put the little lid back on my finger, bandaged it and said it would grow back. It did. But I still have a little horseshoe mark on the tip of my middle finger which I show my sister Mair from time to time.

. . ·· .

Our kitchen had a shiny black range, red floor tiles and a bright green tablecloth of a rough hairy material which I don't like to touch. When we're having a meal with the family, my sister Bob and I have to sit on 'the box', a long chest painted black which holds all the tablecloths, teacloths and towels. My father mashes my potatoes and cabbage together and makes me a castle, but I still don't like it. I have to eat a spoonful or two, though, or I can't have any rice pudding. Dinner times with the whole family are hideously long and I sometimes wish I was a little gipsy girl starving in a wood. My sister Bob and I don't have supper, thank goodness, just two biscuits and a glass of milk. She has to come to bed with me at half past six because I won't go on my own and sometimes she's very cross and calls me a sucky baby - babi swci - but sometimes she reads me a story about Wil Cwac Cwac.

. . . . .

My sister Bob was christened Gwylan, which is Welsh for seagull. Everyone has a different theory of how she came to be called Bob, but I remember being told that it was my brother who had started it, having once had a book called Bob Seagull, and I think this has the ring of truth.

Bob was the introvert of the family, steadily refusing to perform in public and, whenever I did, burying her face in her hands, deeply ashamed.

She had large, bright blue eyes, but for some inexplicable reason my mother would always dress me in blue, her in green, which she detested. This was probably one of the reasons why she often tried to take me down a peg or two. (Another being that I asked for it.)

Even as a small child Bob loved cars and was very upset that we didn't have one. 'A schoolmaster can't afford four children and a car,' my father used to tell her. 'So why didn't you have three children and a car?' she'd ask, looking hard in my direction.

Tib, our black cat, weaves in and out of all my childhood memories. Tib. She deserved a better name. Hannah would have suited her, or Deborah. She was dignified and rather stern.

She was a fine Christian, walking to chapel with my mother every Sunday evening and waiting outside with folded paws until the end of the service. She was seldom idle, but spent her waking hours in profitable labour, catching young rabbits and leverets as well as mice, a goodly multitude. And she also dutifully, yea joyfully, went forth to multiply the earth, bringing unto us two litters of kittens every year.

She had her kittens in the loft over the wash-house, probably to keep them safe from the hot love of my sisters and me. My father would be persuaded to climb up the ladder to report on them. 'What are they like, Dad?' 'Ugly as sin,' was the invariable answer. They were always completely black, sleek and black as little curates.

Tib would carry them down one at a time when their eyes had opened.

There are few things in the world prettier than small black kittens with gentian-blue eyes.

When I first went to Sunday School at three and a half, I learnt the children's hymn, 'Mae ŵyn bach gan yr Iesu,' (Jesus has little lambs) but I insisted that it was, 'Mae ŵy bach gan yr Iesu' (Jesus has a little egg). The thought of this nice, kind man having a little egg, possibly a chocolate egg, pleased me.

I was absolutely distraught when I heard *what they had done to Him*, and ran all the way home, sobbing. My mother used to go to bed on a Sunday afternoon and my father wouldn't let me disturb her, so I had to depend on him for some measure of comfort. My mother would have at least tried to reassure me with a lot of talk about Heaven - where Mamgu was - but all my father said was, 'Well, look at it like this, the poor chap would be dead now in any case'.

On Christmas Day, Bob and I woke in the five o'clock dark to find our rustling stockings. My mother was clever at finding pretty toys for us, with everything fitting neatly and magically into a stocking, tiny six-penny dolls which she would dress and put into little boxes for beds, complete with scraps of material for sheets and blankets, once a little tin pram about four inches long, small rubber balls, tiny paint boxes, note-books and puzzle books and minute packets of sweets.

We were allowed into our parents' bedroom at eight o'clock - not a minute earlier - and soon afterwards my brother Ifan, eighteen or nineteen at this time, came down to open his stocking. And how horrified he was to find the box of chocolates filled with Oxo cubes, onions in the toe instead of an apple and an orange, and instead of the new shirt he'd asked for, a pair of very large pink bloomers. He was often an unsatisfactory brother, demanding quiet when we wanted to play, making trouble if we borrowed even the smallest quantity of his paper and ink, but on Christmas morning he made up for it all.

I remember having a beautiful china doll one Christmas and running along the tiled passage with her in my arms, although my mother had told me over and over again that I was only to play with her in the dining room where there was a carpet. Of course I fell over and her face was smashed to pieces and of course I cried and cried until I had no more breath.

After a decent interval my mother rescued the clothes - white silk dress, green knitted jacket and bonnet - and put them on an old rag doll, Kitty Fawr (Big Kitty), who had once belonged to my sister Mair, an ugly doll with painted lips and eyes and strands of thick black wool for hair. Naturally I threw her to the other side of the room. Later, though, I was sorry I'd been cruel and picked her up and nursed her - and eventually became fond of her. Which was just as well, because I didn't get another china doll for several years.

When my sister Bob went up to Standard Two, she learnt History and I had to repeat after her, 'Nelson was a great sailor. Napoleon was a great soldier'. I felt I was going to like History.

In the Infants, the language had been Welsh, but in Standard Two it was English, so she also taught me to read and write English. I remember having trouble with the silent 'k'. For a long time, I wrote kno for no. I still think it looks more decidedly negative that way. Kno.

. . . . .

Our house was tall and ugly and called Myrtle Villa. The man who'd built it had intended a pair, one each for his two children. Unfortunately one of them had died so he only completed one, which being asymmetric, always looked like a house in mourning for its other half.

My sister Bob and I slept on the top floor in a bedroom overlooking the vegetable garden. In summer, with the window wide open, we could hear my father digging, the rise and fall of his spade steady as heartbeat. After he'd planted potatoes, he'd do a little run along the row to flatten and firm the earth. I loved that. It looked as though he was playing trains.

In the winter Bob and I went to bed with a little oil lamp; she, of course, deputed to carry it up the two flights of stairs. When it was very hard weather we had a Valor stove which cast patterns like bright orange doilies on the ceiling. Sometimes Tib would sneak up and have a nap at our feet, but we could never persuade her to stay long; she was a busy cat with a hundred and one things to attend to.

I remember the summer when I was first allowed to go to meet my sister Bob from school, I think this was when I was getting on for four. One afternoon I'd set off too early and since it was very hot, I sat down to wait for her on the grass verge outside the nearer farm (there were two farmhouses fronting the lane to Llanbadarn, Brynamlwg and Cefnllan, this one was Brynamlwg) and soon I was overwhelmed by sleep. I woke up to find a little girl staring down at me. It shouldn't have been a particularly frightening experience, but somehow it was. Feeling like Goldilocks discovered by the three bears, I burst into tears and didn't stop until Bob arrived to rescue me.

The little girl's name was Freda. I never had the chance to get to know her because her family left Brynamlwg before I started school. But I can still see her little round face staring down at me.

The Waun was a small hamlet a mile from Aberystwyth on the Cardiganshire coast. Now, of course, it's a suburb of the town with neat estates on all the little fields where we played. But I can remember when it was one main road surrounded by countryside, when everyone knew everyone else and everyone got their groceries from The Shop, officially called Hendre Stores, but known to the Waun inhabitants and the inhabitants of several surrounding villages as The Shop. There was no other.

One of the things I remember most was the abundance of wild flowers everywhere, the banks of primroses and violets, the arched branches of dog roses, the daisies and buttercups, the ladysmock all silver-white.

The only things I remember even more vividly than the flowers were the butterflies. On the lane from our house to Llanbadarn we passed a little copse of coniferous and deciduous trees and at certain times, in the best weather, there were clouds of blue butterflies there, tiny ones and larger ones, some as pale as speedwell, some as deeply blue as the midsummer sky over Wales.

Mr and Mrs Arthur ap Gwynn came to live on the Waun in an extraordinary new house, all windows and flat roof. They didn't go to church or chapel - the first heathens I'd encountered - but in spite of that I was allowed to play with their daughter, Nonn, because she was the grandchild of the poet T. Gwynn Jones and my mother thought that made up for it. Nonn had lots of wonderful books and toys, but being at that time an only child, had little notion of sharing. Her North Wales Welsh both fascinated and amused me, it seemed as alien as Chinese, and I used to go about saying 'Fi bia fo, Siân. Dydw i'm isio i chi gyffwrdd ag o, Siân' ('That's mine, Siân. I don't want you to touch it, Siân.') She said Siôn Corn for Santa Clôs and hufen ia for eiscrim, but the thing I found most hilarious was *frog* for frock; I used to imagine her wearing a frog, blue striped or spotted pink.

I thought she was very lucky not to have to go to Sunday School, though I did worry about her being refused entry to Heaven, which seemed a dull place but better than the alternative.

. . . . .

I could see Tib's unborn kittens squirming about in her belly, sometimes a tiny leg thrusting out so that I could all but stroke it. I knew that the big lump at the cow's side was her calf waiting to be born, so the mystery of human birth was soon apparent to me, and I started inspecting every woman I knew.

'Is Mrs Gwynn going to have a new baby?' I asked my mother one day. 'Whoever told you that?' 'I saw it sticking out of her.'

My mother was very tight-lipped; I'd overstepped the mark again, prying into things which only concerned grown-ups. I remember feeling sorry that she was embarrassed about something I found so natural and so fascinating.

. . . . .

My mother's younger sister, my Auntie Maggie, lived in Borth, a village eight miles away. My mother used to visit her for an afternoon every week, and before I started school I used to go with her, travelling free as an under-five.

I loved the bus journey through hills and small villages and wished it would last for ever. The world looked different from the window of a bus, you could see into people's gardens, not just the flower borders which you could see from the road but their washing on the line, the buckets over the rhubarb, the privies around the back: all their private arrangements.

My mother was always happy when she was with her sister, who was very gentle and soft-spoken and an invalid. I had two cousins, Gwenith and Dan, twelve and seven years older, but Dan was often home from school, being 'delicate' like my Auntie Maggie. When he was home, he was made to play Ludo with me. When he wasn't, I used to sit quietly in Auntie Maggie's bedroom, pretending to be playing with Gwenith's old dolls, but really eavesdropping on the sisters' private talk about women's afflictions - including husbands.

Auntie Maggie's husband, my Uncle Tom, was a big genial man, a Maths teacher at Machynlleth County School. He always seemed delighted to see us and never minded making tea for two extra people. He used to cut a huge plateful of the thinnest bread and butter I'd ever seen and there was a selection of exotic shop-made jams to go with it - in our house we only had home-made, which wasn't half as nice.

Though Auntie Maggie wasn't up to making jam, she used to make a huge fruitcake every Saturday; Uncle Tom used to take her the ingredients and she'd sit up in bed, all shawls and scarves, to do the mixing and beating.

The family lived in a big bungalow right opposite the sea. It was called Erwau Glas (Blue Acres). Auntie Maggie herself had drawn up the plans for the bungalow where she, in her bedroom, could be the Queen Bee in the centre of the hive.

Sometimes Auntie Maggie got up from bed because she simply *had* to play the piano. She played the piano better than anyone else because she was an el-r-ey-em. When you were an el-r-ey-em you played Schubert instead of tunes and it lasted *much* longer.

Dan was seven years older than I, but in spite of this a highly satisfactory cousin. Living in Borth with its influx of Birmingham summer visitors, he had acquired a certain sophistication, for instance he said Number One for pi-pi, and it was from him I got my first rude joke. 'I'm going to climb a tree.' 'What tree?' 'Lavat'ry.' But though I practised it often, I could never manage the punchline with his devastating aplomb.

He was tall for his age, and pale, with unruly black hair. When first introduced to ink, his hands looked like the hands of an ink-miner, his shirt cuffs were splattered, and according to my Auntie Maggie, his school books were flooded, oh, not with blots, but with oceans, lakes and rivers of ink.

Although his father was a mathematical wizard, Dan remained stubbornly unmoved by the felicity of the subject and was still having difficulties with take-aways. He walked round his piles of games and comics rather than put them away and never rolled up his school tie at night. I wonder what became of William Brown? My cousin Dan became a Nonconformist minister.

My mother's elder sister, my Auntie Siân, was my favourite. She was a rebel; when she was a young teacher in Cardiff she had been a suffragette. My mother was always begging me to be good, but my Auntie Siân encouraged me to be naughty and to say what I really meant. Once, this was when I was about seven, my Sunday school teacher had written in my autograph album, 'Be good, sweet maid, and let who will be clever', and my Auntie Siân was so incensed by this that she shook me quite hard and said, in English, too, which showed how upset she was, 'Don't you ever be good and sweet. You be a proper devil'. I can still remember how she said it, *'a proper devil'*.

Many years after this, she told me that she'd always been bitter because her five brothers had all been to University, but she, the sixth in the family and a girl, was only allowed to study at home for a teacher's certificate.

My mother was forty-five when I was born and after my birth had a thrombosis which left her very unwell, so her sister Siân, wife of D. J. Williams, the writer and politician, fostered me from the time I was six months old till just after my first birthday. Siân and D. J. were in their forties when they got married, and having no children of their own, became keen to adopt me. My mother, increasingly worried by the tone of their letters, sent my father to fetch me home, but he was persuaded to return without me.

The next day my mother travelled down to their house in Fishguard. At first I clung to D. J. but eventually some early memory must have stirred and I cried to go to her. 'Cer te,' D. J. said crossly. 'Go then.'

'Why did you want to adopt me?' I often asked him, angling for a declaration of undying love.

He'd look at me gravely. 'It was because you could pull faces that terrified everybody,' was all he'd say.

One year my Auntie Siân and my Uncle D. J. spent Christmas with us and we had a very lively time. D. J. put me up on his shoulders so that I should offer a speech of thanks to my mother for the magnificence of the dinner. I got over-excited and wriggled about, he let go of my ankles and I fell over onto the tiled floor and was knocked unconscious.

'They're like two children,' my Auntie Siân said after I'd been revived with something called *sal volatile*. 'One as bad as the other.'

She always pretended to disapprove of all my Uncle D. J.'s naughty ways, but I knew she was really very proud of him. She was even proud when he burned down the bombing school at Penyberth soon afterwards, though my father thought that was *going too far*.

I cried a lot when I heard he'd had to go to prison.

Wormwood Scrubs.

Waldo Williams is one of the greatest Welsh poets of the century. I know that now, but when I was a little girl, he was just a friend of my Uncle D. J.'s, and like him a very childlike person whom I was always having to reprove. For instance when my Auntie Siân wasn't in the room he used to tell my Uncle D. J. rude stories which contained dreadful words like shit, which really upset me, because my Uncle D. J. was bad enough without that.

Sometimes Waldo was asked to keep me company when D. J. and Siân went out to a meeting or to supper with someone, and he never remembered that I was supposed to be in bed by eight *at the very latest* and even when I reminded him, always persuaded me to stay up for one more game. He particularly liked a game called railway tunnels in which you turned the knob of the wireless very fast to see who could produce the best train noise. I couldn't help feeling that it was rather a childish game, but he never seemed to tire of it. 'Listen to the wind,' he used to say. 'Listen to the wind in the telegraph wires.' My Auntie Siân tried to persuade me to call him Uncle Waldo, but how could I? 'No, no, we're just two cousins,' he used to say. 'Dou gender ŷ'n ni.'

Our next door neighbours were called Mr and Mrs Phillips.

Mr Phillips was very old and didn't speak to anyone. He sat in a big wooden armchair by the fire all day, and at the end of his life, slept there too.

Mrs Phillips would sometimes grow tired of his silences and visit us for an hour or two. My mother was always pleased to see her and gave her the best chair, but she would never take a cup of tea. Her skin was brown as an acorn and the channels and cross-channels of her wrinkles were ingrained with dirt; I suppose she had grown too old to wash. She wore a woollen cap and a black and purple pinafore over her black clothes.

She talked to my mother about the old days. She could remember the road being made and our house being built.

She had cataracts on her eyes and she said they made her see 'great landscapes' (landscapes mowr).

Whenever I had a new frock, I would run to show it to Mrs Phillips and she would say I was a bonny girl. Sometimes she would even persuade Mr Phillips to raise his head to look at me.

My sister Mair had a friend called Joan Lewis, one of a large family; four boys, three girls, widowed mother, all very good-looking.

What I remember most clearly about Joan is that she had very painful periods. And Mair, accompanied by me, would stay with her while she suffered, pale as a saint, in the outside lavatory. Of course I was told that she had tummy-ache, but since I eavesdropped exhaustively on my mother and my Auntie Maggie discussing all manner of bodily ailments I knew she was menstruating, 'dod i'w lle', as they called it, 'coming to her place', reaching maturity, perhaps. As a result of this phrase, my polite term for my vagina has always been 'my place'.

It was through Joan Lewis that I got the first hint of what it was to be a female creature with a sweet, distinctive female smell.

My memories are not all of kittens, flowers, butterflies, relatives and friends. I was also aware of *Death* lurking about waiting to strike. Sometimes I'd be engaged with several tragedies before dinner-time: a fly caught in a spider's web, the spider dancing on the high wire of his net to claim it, Tib bringing in a little grey mouse and playing gently with it until it gently expired at her feet, my father seizing the caterpillar that was delicately munching the fringes of a bright green cabbage leaf and squashing it under his boot even as I was listening to it chewing, yet another toad flattened like a yellow leaf on the road. I buried as many as I could of the victims, with a stone or a few flowers to mark the spot. Sometimes our garden seemed nothing but a vast cemetery.

Once, a neighbour died, a young woman called Lily Summersbee. My mother said she was very beautiful. I don't think I'd ever seen her, she'd been ill a long time, but I pictured her lovely dead face and felt very sad. She had TB, 'y pla gwyn' (the white plague).

There was also *Fear*; fear of the dark, fear of noises on the stairs and black creatures with flapping wings.

One day, my cousin Dan and his friend Raymond came to our house for tea. After tea, they and my sister Bob and I were sent out to the garden to play, so that my mother and my Auntie Maggie could have a cosy chat about minor ailments like the change and hot flushes. (It must have been some momentous occasion, perhaps the Urdd Eisteddfod at Aberystwyth, which had brought Auntie Maggie from her bed).

It was twilight and Dan and Raymond decided to play Wolves and Travellers. They, of course, had to be the wolves and they chased after Bob and me, shouting 'Blaidd. Blaidd'. I was terrified. I thought they *were* wolves.

Even now the word *blaidd* seems much more awesome to me than the word 'wolf', showing, I suppose, that one language can never completely replace another, because words carry their weight of associations with them.

One of my greatest fears was of my mother's death, but she promised me that she wouldn't die until I was thirty-five and that comforted me a lot; thirty-five seemed a world away. She also promised that I'd have four children of my own by that time, and I never doubted her. I used to make lists of names: Susan, Jennifer, Diana, Pauline. I didn't want boys.

One morning my father had to go to school in a snow storm. It was unfit for anyone to be out, but he had to open the school in case some children had managed to get there. My mother expected him back within the hour, but he didn't arrive until mid-afternoon; he'd been caught in a blizzard. When he got in, he slumped into a chair unable to say a word. I was sure he was going to die, but my mother put blankets round him and a cup of hot cocoa in his hands and he didn't.

One summer's day, my sister Bob and I found a red
setter.

The way you find a red setter is to walk along a lane
carrying a picnic tea, and a red setter jumps on you and
licks your face and later eats most of your blackberry jam
sandwiches and your chocolate biscuits and when it's
time to go home, bounds along with you, and then
you've found him.

Your father looks at his collar and says he comes all the
way from town and that he'll contact the owner. Bob and
I have to go to bed, crying of course, because (a) we want
to keep him and (b) he's shut up in the shed - because of
Tib, - and whining. Later on, when we're asleep, the
owners come to fetch him.

They're so pleased to get him back that in a few days'
time they send Bob and me a book each as a reward. Not
children's books which cost a shilling or half a crown,
but beautiful grown-up books illuminated in red, blue
and gold which cost *six shillings each*. Mine is *Morte
d'Arthur* by Alfred Lord Tennyson and it's my favourite
book for years and years and years. (Oh, Sir Bedevere,
the best of all my knights.)

We never found another red setter, although we looked
all the time.

One Saturday during the holidays my father had every one of his teeth extracted. (It was something that happened quite frequently at that time; some back tooth might be giving trouble, so, heigh-ho, it was time to have the whole lot out.)

I remember feeling horrified to see him so altered, his nice smile slipping down into a red hole.

. . . . .

I started school officially a few weeks before my fifth birthday. I remember Miss Jenkins, my class teacher, taking me in to Miss Jones who taught the English language infants, so that she should hear how well I could read in both Welsh and English. I remember how I showed off, putting such a weight of expression into sentences like, 'Ro-ver plays with Kitty in the gar-den'. I remember Miss Jones looking at me with some curiosity, but saying nothing. In spite of this, or perhaps because of this, I took to Miss Jones immediately. She had faded sandy hair, a gentle voice and a lost expression.

Miss Jenkins was a teacher of the old school, making the class repeat every new fact over and over again. 'Unwaith eto,' she'd say, 'once more'. But she never meant once more, but once more twenty or fifty times over, which I found unsettling. How could I put up with a teacher who didn't tell the truth?

On my first day at school, I was put to sit by a little girl called Julia Jones who was plump and pretty with soft brown eyes and golden hair. She was only just four and quite a lot smaller than I was. She told me that she had a brother called Billy who'd be meeting her out of school; he was at the County School and his holidays weren't yet over. At first I liked her very much and hoped she would be my best friend.

But at the end of the second or third day I caught sight of Billy. Who was tall and slim with shiny brown skin. Who was beautiful. He picked Julia up by her little plump arms and swung her into the air and I experienced a wave of jealousy that almost knocked me over. For days, for weeks perhaps, I imagined Billy picking me up by the arms and swinging me around. But I was tall and gangly with long thin arms. It wouldn't be the same. I wanted to *be* Julia. So from time to time I used to pinch her quite hard. And at last she told Miss Jenkins who put her to sit with someone else.

. . . . .

On a Thursday afternoon when playtime was over, Miss Jenkins used to read us a story, usually one by the Brothers Grimm or Hans Christian Andersen.

There are many who believe that children learn to confront their fears by hearing about giants and goblins and little dying matchgirls, but I've never been one of them. I started having nightmares, and as though that wasn't bad enough, reverted to wetting the bed, so that my mother told my father that I was to leave Miss Jenkins's class before the Thursday story-hour and go to sit at the back of his classroom, never mind if I did disrupt his lessons.

I don't know how my father managed to square it with Miss Jenkins and I don't care; I escaped those one-eyed ogres and melting tin soldiers for ever.

It was lovely in my father's room, having my first intro-duction to parts of speech and sentence analysis. My father was alarmed but proud when I put up my hand to answer one of his questions. 'Adjective, Sir,' I said. He smiled in rather a self-conscious way, but would often say, 'Adjective, Sir,' to me after that.

. . . . .

I could learn a poem long before anyone else, but I wasn't very good at singing. One day Miss Jenkins listened to us one at a time to find out who was out of tune and afterwards I was asked to sing *very softly* which wasn't much fun.

Another thing I wasn't any good at was handwork. Handwork was raffia. In raffia you made tablemats using three colours and all you did was under, over, under, over, until you'd finished all the raffia on your needle and had to go out to the front for some more. You couldn't even choose a colour. When you wanted red you had to have brown or purple because everybody wanted red. You couldn't even have green.

The hands of the clock didn't seem to move when it was raffia. My mother said it was what they made prisoners do in jail, so I vowed there and then to eschew a life of crime. Bread and water and arrows on your clothes was bad enough without raffia as well.

. . . . .

Even though I've started school, my sister Bob still tries to pass on to me all she's learnt that day. One night she tells me that my drawings are all wrong. I draw green grass at the bottom of my paper and blue sky at the top, with the space we all live in in between. But she's been taught that the sky meets the grass with nothing at all in between them. I'm so disturbed by this concept that my father has to come upstairs to settle the matter. Somehow or other he finds for my sister. I don't begin to understand his explanation, but the sky seems to weigh very heavily on me for a few days.

It's difficult for anyone born after the war to realise what Monday's wash day involved, before the automatic washing machine, the easy-care fabrics and Kleenex. To make things worse, starched tablecloths and table napkins were still used, flannelette nightclothes still worn. Houses had no central heating so men still wore thick vests and long pants, and women, several layers of underclothes; combinations, camisoles and bust bodices and long directoire knickers. And all garments were much too big. A man's shirt, now, is shaped to the body with buttons down the front for easy ironing, then they were great ballooning things, big enough for Michelin man.

I was glad to rush off to school on a Monday, to escape the tin bath full of soaking clothes, the smell and steam of boiling clothes, the earthenware pans of starch and blue with their own sickly smells and the white enamel pan of disgusting handkerchiefs soaking in salt and water.

A girl from school dies; a big girl, I think she was about nine, I think she had diphtheria. Her name was Joan Bannister. The Top Class went to church for the funeral service and the whole school went to the cemetery afterwards. Some of the big boys wore black armbands, some of the big girls held handkerchiefs to their eyes.

You knew about coffins and graves. On sunny afternoons you played in the cemetery, which was on the way home on Cefnllan Hill. Rolling down the grassy slope between the gravestones, it seemed quite a friendly place. But when it was someone you knew the face of, you felt waves of fear, brown and oily as tar in your stomach and you couldn't look at anyone.

The hole in the ground was very deep.

On Sunday there was Chapel. Sometimes you tried to listen to the Reading, especially if it was about God smiting his foes in the Old Testament. During the Prayer, you put your chin on the book-rest of the pew and sat studying the bald heads of the deacons in the Big Seat; brown and shiny, or porridge-white and dry, worst of all white and dry and speckled with yellowish freckles; you thought baldness was a necessary condition of being a deacon, like passing the Scholarship for going to County School. The hymns gave you a chance to stand up and look round and during the sermon you pulled wool off your jumper and your gloves to make a big multi-coloured ball of fluff.

Sunday School was in the vestry. The teachers were two spinster sisters, Lillian and Beatrice Davies, both endearingly dim but very good-natured. We spent the long hour from two to three in rather surprising ways; one year we learnt by heart the names of all the Books of the Old Testament. I quite liked the slow sleepy chanting; a leisurely train journey from Genesis to Diarhebion, but with a definite uphill gradient come Habacuc, Sephaniah, Haggai, Zechariah, Malachi.

There was no particularly noteworthy feature to our vestry except for its lavatory which was the primitive earth type, but with three holes in the seat, one large and two small, considered, even at that time, something of a rarity, certainly worth one or two visits every Sunday.

My mother disliked housework. She was really a frustrated writer; she'd had one or two plays and short stories on the wireless and several one-act plays published. They were written for all-women casts and were particularly valuable for the WIs. Several of them were written for the Waun drama group and performed in the local hall and my sisters and I were allowed to watch the rehearsals. Naturally I knew them all by heart. Their only fault in my eyes was that they had no part for a smart five year old.

The star of my mother's plays was a dark-haired, dark-eyed, middle-aged woman called Rosie James. She could have been another Thora Hird except that she had elderly parents to look after and a farm to run. Women's lives were closely confined in those days.

My sister Bob and I were good friends considering how different we were. I loved performing, showing off, making the maximum fuss about everything; she was reserved, even secretive, and got a lump in her throat if asked to do anything in public. Naturally we had different friends; hers were sedate little girls rather older than she was, mine were absolutely anyone who'd let me play.

When I had chicken pox, though, the only other child home from school with the same illness was out of my class; he wore a handkerchief fastened to his jumper with a safety-pin, which I considered decidedly uncool, and he was still, though a year older than I was, having difficulties with bs and ds.

Anyway, after a day or two on my own, I decided that he might be very slightly better than no one, so one morning I went to call for him. We walked about for a while kicking the grass in the field outside his house and then he wanted to see how I did pi-pi so I showed him and then he showed me. But when I wanted to touch his little bud, the first I'd seen, he ran crying to his mother and I had to go home.

His family left the Waun soon afterwards, but not on my account, I trust.

One summer my father changed houses with another schoolmaster so that both families could have a month-long holiday at minimum expense. We went to Aberporth, a village by the sea only thirty miles away, but a change of scene, as my mother said.

Our family had the better deal; the holiday house had a bathroom and a separate inside lavatory. That's what I remember most clearly about the holiday. Not the miles of golden sands, the warm rock pools and the little pink shells. *But the bathroom. And the lavatory with a chain.*

My sister Bob and I spent the first few days worrying that the family in our house might not remember to feed Tib, but my mother assured us that she'd wind herself round their ankles until they did.

My Auntie Siân came to stay with us because Uncle D. J. was in prison. Wormwood Scrubs. And however much I read to her from my new book, called *Rollicking Times*, it didn't seem to cheer her up.

My brother was spending his time with a girl called Llinos, but we didn't blame him because she had a li-lo.

My sister Mair borrowed my mother's real gold bangle and lost it in the sea and there was a big row about it. She should have *asked* if she could borrow it. (But then my mother would only have said no).

Llinos had platinum blonde hair. Several young women had platinum blonde hair that summer. It looked like yellow, but it was platinum blonde.

. . . . .

Electricity comes to the Waun. What excitement in the Davis household. No more oil lamps, no more blackened funnels to clean, no wicks to trim, nothing but the click of a switch - and let there be light.

My mother has a day out buying lampshades; sixpenny ones from Woolworths for the top floor bedrooms, parchment ones with raffia stitching for the first floor, marbled glass bowls suspended on chains for the dining room and the study, octagonal white glass for the kitchen. What for the sitting room where my father listens to the wireless, now converted to electric power? I can't remember, but something rather distinguished no doubt.

My mother has an electric iron. No more waiting for a glowing fire, no more spitting on the iron to test the temperature, but a dial to turn to silk, rayon, cotton. My mother has an electric stove and an electric kettle and an electric fire for her bedroom and she'll be happy for ever and ever.

· · · · ·

Granma comes to stay with us in September. Granma is my father's mother and she wears little black boots. She likes to sit out in the garden peeling apples or slicing beans and doesn't want to be a trouble to anyone. My father calls her Ma.

Granma lives in a town called Port Talbot with my Auntie Florrie, my Uncle Stan and my cousin Dorothy. My cousin Dorothy is the same age as my sister Mair. Dorothy is always *pleased* to wear the clothes that Granma makes for her, but my sister Mair *won't* and that's that.

Granma brings us books about little girls whose mothers are dead and whose fathers *Drink*. Usually the children die at the end and hear a sweet voice welcoming them to Heaven. My sister Bob and I cry buckets every time we read them. Which makes my father very angry.

When Granma goes back on the train to Port Talbot, my father puts the books on a bonfire in the garden and we cry buckets again. 'Your mother's books! You're burning your own mother's books!' But he has no shame.

. . . . .

Coedybryn, the village in South Cardiganshire where I was born, was very important in my early life. My mother's father had once been the minister of a chapel near by, so the area was my mother's home and we often visited it. From here you could see the Freni Fawr, the northernmost peak of the Preseli mountains, which have remained for me the most atavistic and mysterious of mountains.

The most important person in Coedybryn was Nan; Hannah Rees, Brynffynnon, who was big and pretty with black curly hair and a faint moustache, a lovely laugh and a big, warm personality. She always referred to herself in the third person. 'Ody chi'n dod i gal cino da Nan heddi?' ('Are you coming to dinner with Nan today?') Yes, please.

Nan had always worked at home on her father's farm, but she was a nurse by nature and was always called on when there'd been a really sensational accident on one of the local farms. She used to describe the victims she'd nursed, 'No one would recognize any part of him'. My mother would beg to be spared the worst details, but Bob and I would listen, wide-eyed.

Both my grandfathers had died before I was born, so Nan's father, Elias Rees, took over the vacant role, and I adored him. He smoked a pipe, sat me on his knee and would recite, nice and slowly, all the nursery rhymes and folk rhymes he knew and would then be ready to start all over again - and again. I remember how I would push my fingers into his big white beard and stare through his black spectacles into his almost blind eyes. He used to give me extra-strong mints and blow tobacco smoke into my hair. He smoked the strongest shag tobacco; my mother said that as a toddler I always smelled like an old man.

This was one of his rhymes:

Y bore pan ddel	When morning arrives
Y ceiliog a gân	The cockerel will crow
Y ci bach a ddawnsia	The little dog dance
O gwmpas y tân	And the fire will glow
A minnau a godaf	And I shall arise
Os byddaf yn iach	Be it sunny or grey
I dynnu y mwgyn	And light up my pipe
Drwy'r fwgen ddu fach.	To greet the new day.

How difficult it is to capture the sweetness and dignity of a tough old farmer, grown too old to work.

Nan loved us all, all the extended family, extravagantly. My mother, always romantic about her family - 'teulu Brynhawen' - said it was because she'd once been in love with my Uncle Wil, but when he'd gone away to college and got engaged to my Auntie Nesta, she'd had this abundance of love going spare and had showered it on his family; which, if true, would certainly denote great magnanimity.

When Nan died, Uncle Wil wrote this englyn in her memory:

Gloyw iawn yw ein dagrau - yn arwyl
bun dirion, hael fendith.
A byw loes ei rhoi i blith
gwynion dywys Bryngwenith.

Dazzling are our tears - for her,
a gentle woman, greatly blest.
A bitter wound to lay her
with Wheat-hill's white harvest.

(Wheat-hill is the literal translation of Bryngwenith, the name of her chapel, where my grandfather had once been minister.)

· · · · ·

My uncle Wil, the poet Wil Ifan, was a lovely, warm-hearted man who looked at you over his large nose and made everything he said sound funny. He hadn't wanted to be a minister but a country postman and when he preached he always had terrible headaches so that his sermons were nice and short. He painted a picture or wrote a poem to the glory of God every day, so I felt sorry he had to preach as well and wear his collar back to front.

I didn't like my Uncle Jack so much, he would often trap me into saying things he could then make fun of. But I loved this story about him:

My grandmother was taking my mother and my Auntie Maggie for a few days' holiday and he had promised to be at the station to see them off. But he'd recently begun teaching and was delayed. The train was already drawing out when he arrived, but he managed to throw a little packet into the compartment, where it landed at Mamgu's feet. And inside she found all his first month's wages.

That story made me almost ready to forgive his hurtful teasing. I especially liked the bit about the packet landing *at Mamgu's feet*. I made my mother repeat that over and over again.

· · · · ·

My mother's eldest brother, my Uncle Dai, had married the daughter of a very rich farmer. She was fifteen years his senior, but it meant that he could give up his teaching job in London where he'd always been unhappy. His wife was called Ffebi, which is Welsh for Phoebe. She died - of cancer - before I was born, but like everyone else in the extended family I benefited from her inheritance: Pengelly, a Georgian farmhouse set in the lush acres of South Cardiganshire.

As Christians yearn for Heaven, the Jews for the Promised Land and the Muslims for Mecca, our family set our sights on Pengelly, where life was quiet, ordered and luxurious. It had a dining room with a round table large enough for Arthur and his knights, a vast bathroom, great feather beds and old oak chests and presses. Of course we could only visit occasionally, and on a strict rota, I imagine. But oh, the porridge and cream, the chestnut trees, the primroses in the orchard, the cats and the calves and feeding the chickens and the way things smelled - of plenty, I suppose.

As well as plenty, Pengelly had Ann; Ann Jones, housekeeper and cook. She had been with Auntie Ffebi all her life and had transferred her affections to my Uncle Dai - Mister Ifans - and all his clan.

Ann had a very high sing-song voice and liked to explain in the greatest detail how things were done and always had been done on the farm; how many Christmas cakes were baked, how many puddings boiled, how much money put aside for 'calennig' when the lads from the neighbouring farms came round to greet them on New

Year's Day, the first arriving between three and four, what food was provided for the harvest supper, down to the last slice of ham.

She didn't make a fuss of children, had little to say to them. All the same I found her fascinating; her way with words, the rise and fall of her thin voice, her invariable courtesy, particularly towards my father whom she would always address in halting English, however much he insisted he could follow her Welsh perfectly well.

After being a widower for ten years, the farm beginning to lose money, my Uncle Dai remarried an even richer woman; fifteen years younger than himself this time and called Audrey Dorothea Loxdale Basil-Jones. She was the daughter of a former bishop of Saint David's, but never mind, she was a charming woman who adored Uncle Dai. Even though he always called her Ffebi.

The welcome for us all at Pengelly remained as warm as ever, but under the new dispensation, my mother was worried about our shabby pyjamas and cardboard suit-cases so she made other arrangements for my sister Bob and me, and these proved equally delightful.

. . . . .

Miss Jones lived in a small cottage about half a mile from Coedybryn. She was about fifty when I remember her, tall and angular with grey hair in an untidy bun. She was a seamstress, going round the farms making curtains or stitching worn sheets side to middle.

She was delighted to have my sister Bob and me to stay for two or three weeks in the summer holidays, she thought it a much pleasanter way of earning a few pounds.

Why we should have been so happy with her I'm not quite sure. We'd always lived in the country, but in a big solid house in a village; being in Miss Jones's cottage seemed like camping in a field. At the open window of our tiny bedroom we could hear, as well as see, dozens of rabbits chewing the juicy grass. There was no other sound, no cars, no people.

And Miss Jones didn't seem to us as grown-up as other grown-ups. She looked staid and harmless, but she had

wicked eyes and a wicked laugh. In the evenings she would wander round the fields setting rabbits free from snares, in the daytime she didn't do much but collect sticks. We didn't have meals as we knew them, none of the things we disliked, just a little boiling of peas or beans now and then, some stewed apples, some biscuits or buns, strong tea instead of milk.

The well outside Miss Jones's cottage dried up in summer so we had to carry every drop of drinking water from the pump in the village. There was certainly none to spare for washing; we wiped our hands on a flannel dipped in the almost empty rain butt and waved them in the air afterwards to get rid of the slightly stale smell.

Miss Jones had several cats which she'd rescued from snares and traps, some of them limping about on three legs. 'If it wasn't for the cats we'd have milk in our tea,' she'd say sadly, and we had to assure her that we liked blowing on it.

She didn't like men, especially farmers who were so cruel to their animals. She was glad she had never married, though she often said she would have dearly liked to be a sea captain's widow.

I've always been surprised that my mother, a stickler for regular meals, brown bread and butter, milk puddings and early bedtimes, should have trusted us to Miss Jones who let us do exactly as we pleased.

Later, she seemed to resent the affection I still felt for Miss Jones - who after all was not family - pointing out that we'd only stayed with her for two or three summers.

But Miss Jones, with her deep gruff voice and startling pronouncements, 'Aren't men lucky to go bald. I'd do anything to lose my hair,' exists in the world of the imagination where many of my most decent and honourable relations never intrude.

. . . . .

The day she'd got engaged to my father, my mother had bought herself a Singer sewing machine - and a shrewd investment it turned out to be. She could make me or my sister Bob a dress from a shilling remnant, and it would be ready the next day. She usually dispensed with the optional extras like collars and pockets, the two sleeves might not have quite the same amount of puff, never mind, a new dress was a new dress and the materials she snapped up at Howells' July sales were always eye-catching; she was particularly fond of bright blue and deep violet, the vibrant colours of the Arts and Crafts movement, fashionable when she was young.

I loved the steady whirr of the sewing machine and longed to turn the little black and gold handle, but I was never allowed to: dressmaking was a serious grown-up occupation.

Miss Bronwen Jenkins, my teacher, pretends to admire my new dress. 'Isn't it beautiful,' she tells Miss Jones at playtime. 'Isn't it *well-made*.' She thinks I don't understand sarcasm, but I do, though perhaps I don't know the word. Miss Jones is kinder and doesn't feel the need to diminish me because I'm the headmaster's daughter.

Luckily, I'm quite difficult to put down. I have murderous thoughts for a minute or two, then I'm ready for the fray again. After playtime I shall interrupt Miss Jenkins every few minutes with difficult questions. 'Who made God?' was one I thought of last week.

Miss Jenkins's jumpers are perfectly knitted so that they look ready-made, but she often gets flustered by my questions. 'You don't need to know that in Standard One,' she tells me.

. . . . .

I was often sick and unable to go to school. I quite enjoyed it after that first day when I felt I was in a hot tunnel with distorted voices coming at me from either end.

I'd be moved to my parents' bedroom on the first floor so that I was within reach. There were two Chinese paintings over the fireplace in that room, trees and bridges and pagodas, and when I was ill I could see frightening faces in them. My mother didn't need to take my temperature, I knew I was better when the faces went away.

When I wasn't allowed to read - and in our house, when you had a temperature you weren't allowed to read - other entertainments would be provided. My father would be sent upstairs to recite 'The Pied Piper of Hamelin' which he'd learned - all fifteen long stanzas of it - as a boy. (I didn't really like it, it made me feel uncomfortable, but I appreciated it.) My brother Ifan would occasionally look in and croon one or two of the popular songs, 'Bye-bye Blackbird' and 'The Lullaby of Broadway'. And Mair and Bob would be sent upstairs to help me with jigsaw puzzles, which I hated then and still do.

My mother, having been a teacher herself, had no very high regard for school. Whenever I was unwell with either a recognised childhood illness or a mysterious fever I was kept home for weeks at a time. Of course there were no antibiotics then and I suppose the dangers were real enough. 'She should be at school,' my father used to say, but with little hope.

After a week in bed, the kitchen seemed exciting new territory and reclaiming my crayons and paints and glitterwax as good as Christmas.

When my mother decided I was well enough to venture outside, two inches taller and pale as porridge, there were three neighbours I regularly visited. Mrs Winstanley used to enjoy or at least tolerate hearing the long poems by Eifion Wyn or Robert Louis Stevenson which I'd learnt during my convalescence, Mrs Pugh would give me wool to unravel or her sewing box to tidy, keeping conversation to a minimum, but Mrs Lewis used to sit down and talk to me as an equal.

She had white silky hair and a large, calm face. When I got up to leave she always said, 'Os raid I chi fynd?' ('Do you really have to go?') I was proud of my grown-up friends, though I always forgot them as soon as I was back at school.

Occasionally my temperature remained high for so long that Dr Ellis was called in, a real storybook doctor with black suit, stiff white collar and gold watch-chain across his large expanse of waistcoat. Once, after peering at my tonsils and tapping my chest, he took a blood test and a few days later we got the result, which was this: partially positive para-typhoid. I was well again by this time, but had to go to the Isolation Hospital for four weeks. It was a very boring time, but I was sustained by my sense of importance. 'Partially positive para-typhoid,' I said to myself over and over again.

I was the only person in the ward. In an adjoining ward there was a little fair-haired boy called Ronnie Miller who had scarlet fever. When we were allowed out of bed we used to wave at each other. (We met at the County School years later but never referred to our earlier encounter in pyjamas.)

My mother came to see me every afternoon, walking two miles each way - isolation hospitals were really isolated, this one was along a cliff path, far from a bus route - but she never managed to supply me with enough books to fill the hours and hours I had to spend on my own. My father used to do his best, sending me all the travellers' samples that came his way, *Science for Beginners*, *Travel in the Desert*, *Life in a Medieval Village*, *Women of the Bible*, everything was welcome.

One of the young nurses, feeling sorry for my selection of reading matter, brought me a job lot of books from her digs. Some of them were by a local author called Countess Barcynska, books of high romance, giving me a first insight into all manner of intriguing diversions. Receptive to all new ideas, I couldn't wait to grow up.

. . . . .

When I came out of hospital, I found that my father had put up a swing in the garden, a good strong swing that hung from a thick branch of a sycamore tree near the road.

When my friends came to play, I always insisted on my turn - twenty goes each - usually managing to go higher than anyone else. But when I was on my own, I just sat on the seat, my feet paddling a bit on the grass, hardly swinging at all. It was the best place for thinking things out, trying to understand grown-ups, how they were so cross if they thought you were cheeky and then repeated what you'd said when people came to tea, why some things made you laugh while other quite similar things twisted your stomach and made you cry, most of all trying to understand who you were.

My favourite colour is blue. My favourite month is May. My favourite animal is a tiger. My favourite bird is a wren. My lucky number is five. I like reading and painting and learning poetry. But what then? What else?

. . . . .

I loved picking blackberries. I suppose part of the pleasure was the idea of getting something for nothing, but it was much more than that. While out picking I'd often feel in a near-trance; nothing in the world except hedge, sky, the thin autumn smells and the sun at my back.

I pitied the town people who seemed satisfied with the meagre crop of harsh, reddish berries on the roadside. I knew every field, every bramble bush, all the boggy places where the fruit was ripe and juicy, ready to tumble plumply into my basket. I picked until my fingers were stained purple and my bare legs scratched and sore; nothing could stop me. One September my mother made fifty pounds of blackberry jam.

Blackberries are said to be devil's fruit in October; my father thought that could be due to the increased likelihood of snakes in the hedges. I never came across a snake, though I was often startled by frogs and toads jumping out at me. Once I found a sheep's skull and once an old black kettle.

There are few better smells in the world than a blackberry tart fresh from the oven.

. . . . .

I used to roam for miles, well for a mile or two anyway, in my search for the first primroses, the white primroses and the pink, the white violets and the little purple heartsease, but such was life in those days that I came to no harm.

There was an elderly man, though, one summer, who called me over to him and tried to show me his willy; eccentric behaviour, and sufficiently disturbing to report to my mother.

She took a deep breath and said he was *a very nice man*, she emphasised this, whose mind had been sadly adrift since the death of his wife and the arrival of a daughter-in-law who bullied him. But he had once been *a faithful member of our chapel*, so I was to feel sorry for him and not tell anyone about his silly behaviour or make fun of him. I was to hurry past him, but waving cheerily so that he didn't feel slighted.

So that was that. I now knew how to deal with him, and indeed with any man who might behave in such a *silly* fashion.

I'm happy to say that I never again had any similar trouble, so never had the occasion to put theory into practice. I can't help thinking, though, that the cheery waving would be enough to disconcert any sexual deviant.

. . . . .

My mother loved the auction sales which were held in Aberystwyth on the first Wednesday of the month. She got many bargains there, a set of slightly unsteady Victorian chairs, five shillings for four, a handsome deckchair with a canopy, sixpence, a string hammock which gave us pleasure for years, one shilling. Best of all, though, and a regular purchase, was the tin bath crammed full of books for sixpence.

Sometimes there'd be a wonderful selection of old annuals, 'Playbox' and 'Jingles' and 'Girls' Own'; at other times we had to be satisfied with musty old volumes with titles like *The Reverend Obadiah Jones, his Life and Reflections* and *Famous Welsh Missionaries of the Nineteenth*

Century, Leviticus Revealed, and *Whence Now, Lord?* But there were always one or two worthwhile books among them.

It was in a most unpromising lot that I discovered *Daddy Longlegs* by Jean Webster and *Wee Macgregor,* both of which I treasured for years.

A sixpenny bath of books was generally a pretty good buy.

. . . . .

Our family had once had a dog - Pero - but that was before my time. My two sisters had apparently cried with such operatic abandon when he'd died that my father had sworn never to have another. ('Not while I'm alive,' he'd announce cheerfully, evoking, of course, the inevitable response, 'How soon after you're dead?' which he quite enjoyed).

To make up for this cruel deprivation, my sister Bob and I lavished a great deal of affection on an old, chained-up, half-blind sheepdog called Prince, who used to thump his tail with embarrassment as he backed into his kennel to get away from us. The other dogs in the village were corgis, noisy and unfriendly.

The only horse we knew well was one we met every Thursday on our way home from school, pulling a wagon piled high with brooms and buckets and other ironmongery. Its owner, a tall, thin, grey-haired woman, also delivered paraffin to all the neighbouring villages, and usually wore two top coats, several scarves - one crossed over her chest - and a man's hat. But however cold and tired she might be, she always stopped to let us pat the horse which had a sweet, sad face very like hers. We used to feed it grass which it would snuffle up from our hands with warm, rubbery lips. We worried about its hard life and always resolved to save it one of our Saturday sweets - but never quite managed it.

I suppose there were more cows than cars making their way through the village at that time. I admired the way they swayed from side to side, refusing to be hurried, but found their casual way of dealing with the natural functions rather less attractive. Close to, they blew at you and seemed large as buses.

One of my mother's brothers, Uncle Eben, had died in the Great War. He served with the Artists' Rifles and was killed at Arras in 1917 in the same battle as Edward Thomas.

Before the war, while teaching in London, my Uncle Eben had married a French governess called Juliette Lasarre, who still lived in London. I can only remember one occasion when she visited us.

Being such an important guest, she'd been put in my parents' bedroom and it was by accident that I called in on her, finding her in their bed. 'Do you know who I am?' she asked me. 'Yes,' I said firmly, 'you're Granma.' She managed to laugh, but I never lived that down: she had the reputation for extreme French chic.

It was probably because of this insult that she took to sending me hideous dresses, made for me with her own fair French hands. They were of thick silk or crêpe de chine, and *smocked*. They had *dropped waists* and *flounces*. It was a punishment to have to wear them on a Sunday, though my mother did her best to persuade me that they made me look like Princess Margaret Rose.

There were often bands of gypsies in the books I read, but I don't remember many in real life, certainly no colourful caravans and tripod fires, only the occasional dark-haired women in purple and black, often with babies in their arms, who came to the door to sell pegs and sprigs of white heather. My mother bought their pegs, but always declined - daughter of the Manse that she was - to have her fortune told.

I remember the whine of their dark voices. I was frightened of them, didn't they, after all, steal children? 'Nonsense,' my father said, 'they have too many of their own. You're absolutely safe.' But I never quite believed him.

There were a great many tramps in rural Wales before the war; small, grey-haired, grey-bearded men who walked slowly along the roads looking at their boots. One would like to think that some of them were free spirits, only wanting to commune with nature, but more likely they were the dispossessed with no other way open to them. In our village, where most people were poor, they seemed to be accepted quite kindly, almost as members of the community, probably because they'd learned to ask for so little. They'd knock at a door, 'Just a spoonful of tea, lady,' they'd say, passing her a chipped enamel can. At the next house, 'Some boiling water, lady?' and when this was forthcoming, 'And perhaps a spoonful of sugar?' At the next house they'd ask a slice of bread, at the next, a lump of cheese, so that everyone could feel pleasantly charitable and hardly at all worse off. I was never at a house where a tramp was refused the little he asked.

My mother would sometimes find an old coat or pair of trousers discarded by my father for one she thought particularly deserving - or perhaps particularly ragged - and he would put it on in the outhouse, leaving his own in a neat bundle at the door.

An interesting fact: tramps always came to the back door, gypsies to the front.

My sister Mair left home to be a nurse in London, beginning her training at the Evelina Hospital for Sick Children in Southwark.

I don't remember her leaving, the taxi taking her to the station; perhaps I was at school. What I remember is the tension in the house beforehand, my mother's indignation and sheer disbelief at the list of garments to be purchased - a dozen of everything, dresses, aprons, caps, cuffs - and the emptiness in the house after she'd gone.

I remember crying when I realized that I wouldn't see her again until she'd finished her preliminary training in six months' time. But my mother insisted that we were *very lucky*. In the old days when one of the family went away to London, they might never come back. She then recited a very sad poem which I've never succeeded in tracking down, 'Mae John yn mynd i Lunden' (John is going to London). The mother packing his clothes feels that the large wooden chest is the coffin bearing him away. That made me cry even more. My mother's cure was often worse than the disease.

My brother Ifan was at college in Aberystwyth and still lived at home. I'd recently got into trouble for painting over one of his essays. The sheets of paper had been written on, on both sides, so I'd assumed they'd been finished with; a very natural error.

And then it was the war. There'd been talk of it for months, my parents listening to the six o'clock news every evening and shaking their heads and sighing. And then it was come.

My father became an air-raid warden, his first task to find homes for the evacuees coming to the area. *Evacuee* was my first new word, with *gas mask* a close second. We heard practice sirens, the warning siren and the all-clear - and I didn't like either.

I don't suppose war affected us very much in rural west Wales, except that my brother was of call-up age and my parents were deeply worried about him. *Conscientious objector* was another new phrase, heard very often in our house because that's what Ifan had decided to become, my mother in favour, my father not, with tired, edgy arguments for and against.

One of my early war memories - though it must have been at least a year later - is my father taking me out to the garden very late one night, so that I should hear the drone of the German war planes flying overhead on their way to bomb Liverpool; a hundred strong he said they were.

'You'll always remember this sound,' he said.

It wasn't the outbreak of the Second World War, though, that marked the end of my childhood innocence, but a small, local affair.

I had a friend called Davy Rice who lived on the nearby farm, Brynamlwg, and I often played with him after school or on a Saturday.

One afternoon he led me, with no malice intended, I'm sure, to a shed where his father was slaughtering a cow. I remember the shot of the gun, the huge thud of the cow's fall, the trickle of dark blood. And Davy's father turning to us and smiling.

I ran home, silent at first, but as I got to the back door, started to scream and went on screaming, my hands over my ears, until my mother and even my father became alarmed. When I eventually stopped, I still wouldn't or couldn't say anything at all. At last my sister Bob came home from a piano lesson in town and guessed what had happened; she had once seen something far worse concerning two calves which I can't even now write about.

I hadn't known. For all that I was often said to be too smart for my own good, I hadn't known what meat was. 'Animals are only animals,' I used to be told, but I couldn't accept it and still can't. 'Why are you a vegetarian?' people ask me, and when they do I can still feel the sickening chill of that afternoon.

That day everything changed; the sky darkened, I became nervous and suspicious, always fearing the unexpected horror, never again completely at ease with my world.

Also from Honno

NOT SINGING EXACTLY
The Collected Stories of Siân James
with an introduction by Katie Gramich

Women awake to all sorts of realisations in *Not Singing Exactly*: awareness of love, of deceit, of loss, of the passing of time - realisations which change their lives for ever. Set against backgrounds which range from West Wales in the forties to Hampstead in the seventies, these stories bring together the best of Siân James' short stories over a twenty-year period, showing the full range of her subtle gifts as a storyteller.

'She writes with grace, as to the manner born.'
- Susan Hill, *The Times*

Winner of the Arts Council of Wales
Book of the Year Award

ISBN 1 870206 18 5
£6.95

About Honno

Honno Welsh Women's Press was set up in 1986 by a group of women who felt strongly that women in Wales needed wider opportunities to see their writing in print and to become involved in the publishing process. Our aim is to publish books by, and for, the women of Wales, and our brief encompasses fiction, poetry, children's books, autobiographical writing and reprints of classic titles in English and Welsh.

Honno is registered as a community co-operative and so far we have raised capital by selling shares at £5 a time to over 350 interested women all over the world. Any profit we make goes towards the cost of future publications. We hope that many more women will be able to help us in this way. Shareholders' liability is limited to the amount invested, and each shareholder, regardless of the number of shares held, will have her say in the company and a vote at the AGM. To buy shares or to receive further information about forthcoming publications, please write to Honno:

'Ailsa Craig',
Heol y Cawl,
Dinas Powys,
Bro Morgannwg
CF64 4AH

HONNO AUTOBIOGRAPHY

Struggle or Starve:
Women's lives in the South Wales
valleys between the two World Wars
edited by Carol White and
Sian Rhiannon Williams

Drawing on the memories of those who were girls and young women during the inter-war period, *Struggle or Starve* vividly recreates the lives of working class women at a time of hardship and poverty. It mingles fragments of reminiscence by previously unpublished writers with extracts from published autobiographies - some long out of print - to portray women's struggle, not just for survival but for dignity, recognition and wider opportunities. Different voices combine to create a picture of a way of life which, though gruelling and often dispiriting, was nevertheless illuminated by the warmth of family ties and friendship.

The critical introduction situates these women's individual experiences within the wider social and political context of a period of mass unemployment and labour unrest, when the only real choice open to the majority of Valleys women was struggle - or starve.

This is a delightful book. It is moving, poignant, funny and a very good historical record.
Emeritus Professor Deirdre Beddoe,
University of Glamorgan

1 870206 25 8   £9.95

HONNO MODERN FICTION

Of Sons and Stars
by
Catherine Merriman

Judith was undressing on Friday night in front of her long bedroom mirror when she realized - with a shock that momentarily paralysed her - that she had become invisible.

Bikers partying in a remote mountain pub; an Englishman in search of mustard in a quiet Welsh village; a housewife whose perfectly ordinary life suddenly becomes very strange indeed ... Catherine Merriman's stories take everyday reality and give it a twist and a spin, transforming it into something bright, shiny and with a definite edge.

The first of Catherine Merriman's three highly praised novels, *Leaving the Light On* (Gollancz/Pan), won the Ruth Hadden Memorial Award. Her first collection of short stories, *Silly Mothers* (Honno), was shortlisted for the Welsh Book of the Year Award.

I would say this author is born to write.
Lynne Reid Banks

1 870206 27 4   £5.95